SUCCESSFULLY PROGRAMMING YOUR MIND

Controlling Your Mind's Programming
Systems Can Change Your Life

ALLEN M. DAUGHERTY

BALBOA.PRESS
A DIVISION OF HAY HOUSE

Balboa Press books may be ordered through booksellers or by contacting:

Balboa Press
A Division of Hay House
1663 Liberty Drive
Bloomington, IN 47403
www.balboapress.com
844-682-1282

Print information available on the last page.

ISBN: 978-1-9822-5965-5 (sc)
ISBN: 978-1-9822-5966-2 (e)

Balboa Press rev. date: 11/30/2020

Contents

Preface vii

Chapter 1   The Input...1
Chapter 2   The Processor...7
Chapter 3   Sorting.. 17
Chapter 4   The Folders 23
            •   Important – Not Important...............23
            •   Want – Need......................................26
            •   Now – Later..28
            •   Fast – Slow 30
            •   Relationships – Associations..............36
            •   Conscious – Subconscious.................39
            •   Trust – Doubt 42
            •   Self – Others 44
Chapter 5   Accessories 49
            •   Caution 49
            •   Sub-Sorting 51
            •   Memory... 54
Chapter 6   Viruses 59
            •   Regrets 59
            •   Bitterness – Hatred............................ 60
            •   Discouragement 62

Conclusion 65

Preface

I am sure you have read many things and have heard many illustrations on how similar the brain, (our mind) is to a computer. This book will use the computer as an illustration of the things that go on in our minds that can be examined and controlled for the best possible outcomes in life. This is not a technical book on computers for one major reason; I don't know much about computers. Secondly, it's not meant to be a deep dive into the field of psychology. It is just a very simple approach to understanding how our mind works and can be trained to work.

Our mind is a wonderful thing that can produce happiness and success. It can also be destructive, cruel and cause us great pain. What you do, what you say, and how you live are governed by actions created in your mind. A great truth is (and basically the purpose of this book) that you can control your mind. For example, others can influence its thoughts by teachings, examples, and various means of communication but in the end; it's our mind that determines how we think, act, react, and live.

Nothing in this book will be a huge, newsworthy revelation, however with all my books, I try to present several truths that will help you be the best that you can be. There will be times while reading that you will stop and say, 'yes, that's so true' or 'Wow, I never thought of it like that'. It's a book full of reminders of how your mind works and how you can leverage all that it has to benefit your life.

Although we are presenting a serious subject, you may also see a bit of humor. I discovered that humor can often help us read and digest material as well as things that occur in our lives. Read it carefully and highlight truths that are important to you. Use the things that you learn, and they will be imbedded even deeper into your nature.

I have been in the medical field for over 46 years. I have done that because I love helping people. That is also why I write. I may be a bit naive, but I do believe that every human being has an inner desire to help others. Some people never let that bubble to the top, but I am hoping that this book will help you, and you in turn can help others.

Parents, as the role model for your children in their very impressionable years, the truths in this book may help you develop some things in your home that will benefit your children throughout their lifetimes. BELIEVE ME, it is much easier to mold them correctly now than to mend them later. Okay, let's get started and see if we can figure out, 'What's the mater with our brains?' Mater….. get it. Brain mater???? Layers of the brain?? Okay, so maybe not so many attempts at humor.

Just a reminder, this is not a book on computer usage. I associated some of the computer terms for the processes our mind undergoes. Please don't throw it away because a real computer processor doesn't do what I am saying it does in the mind. Be gentle with me, I'm just trying to get some great truths across.

Chapter 1

The Input

As you know, computers can only have in them what is put in. You say, 'Well, when I got mine it already had tons of stuff in it.' Yes that is true, but the hardware and any software that was in the computer were already programmed in there by the company. You are correct though. We are born with some basic instincts that develop in different ways throughout our lifetimes.

For example, no one has to teach an infant to cry when they are hungry, need changed, or just want some attention. It is a part of their internal hardware. Yes, it came already installed in the baby. I once saw a cartoon where twins were sitting in a playpen. One of them said, "Watch this. WHAAAAAAAAAA!" They hear a thump, thump, thump, thump up the hall and Mom appeared. They both smiled.

As children get older, they find more mature ways of achieving the same goals. 'Mom, I'm hungry; Mom, I'm thirsty, Mom, I have to go to the bathroom, Mom I ....' Sound familiar Moms?

Later, we will discuss some of the things that are already installed but first, we will look at the things that we install or allow to be installed. There are several ways to import stuff into your computer. There are ports, CD Drives, internet connections, Apps, and others. (Again, please do not laugh at my vast knowledge of computers.)

The brain also has various points of entry. We are going to discuss the two most important ones and those are the eyes and the ears; the things we see and the things we hear.

To further divide our discussion, we are going to look at the controllable and uncontrollable things that our minds may encounter. In other words, the things that we are going to be exposed to regardless of our desires, and the things we permit to be imported.

Many years ago, I was standing in line with my son in a store and the man behind me used the F word. I did not want my son to hear that because I didn't want him to think it was acceptable to talk that way, but I had no control. I did ask the man to please not cuss with my son present. He kindly apologized and didn't cuss again.

On the other hand, we had a rule in our house that no one used foul language. We did not watch shows on TV nor listen to music that had used foul language. I was trying to manage what was going into their computers. It sure is a much more difficult battle to fight in 2020. This book is not on raising children, so I will stop there. I think you get the point. We can't control some exposures but what we can control, we should.

We do have a couple of unique WARNING devices that tells us that the information coming in may contain something that could be harmful to our computer. With all the hackers and computer viruses out there, we have to be careful what we allow to import in. Our mind is the same way. One of our biggest allies in this defense is our *conscience*. It alerts us when we are introduced to things that go against what we believe to be right. The partner of our conscience is *conviction* or what I call, our *character.* Basically, character is our beliefs producing our lifestyle. Our conscience whispers 'Don't do it' and our character says 'I won't do it'.

If you believe pornography is wrong, something inside your computer flashes a warning notice when you are exposed to it (conscience) and you refuse admittance (character). If you don't believe it's good to listen to vulgar, suggestive music, do not allow it to download into your mind when you hear it. These are some very defined examples but there are other, more subtle things that we need to watch for as well.

I believe that all men are created equal. The same, no, of course not. If everyone was just like me, we would be in big trouble. Don't read into that, the same goes for you. (I was going to say Ha! Ha! But nowadays it's LOL) When I hear others make horrible remarks about a race, religion, or nationality, I do not let it download in my mind. My conscience says, 'That's just not right!' My character agrees, and it is not admitted.

I hear and start to read stuff all the time that never remains in my mind. 'There is no God; government should be abolished; we should disband the police force', and so much more.

I am just trying to say that your mind needs protection like an anti-virus program. Your conscience and your character will do the job if they are allowed to. As we will discuss later, what comes out of a computer can only be a result of what is in the computer. If you want your life to produce good, then guard what goes into it.

On the other hand, there are so many great things to fill up a lot of memory in our minds. There are good books to read and good music to listen to. I have seen many books that have a thought or meditation for the day. Something positive and uplifting to get you going. Books and audios that motivate you to reach out for your goals and accomplish them. There are also several radio stations that broadcast inspirational thoughts and positive perspectives.

Sometimes, just looking at the beautiful things around us helps our mind to relax and enhances our positive outlook on life. I love looking at the sunrise and sunset over the ocean. As you are being mesmerized by that picture, your ears take in the crashing of the waves on the beach. Let's just say, I frequently go there in my mind in the middle of a hectic day and it does wonders.

Education is a wonderful way to enrich your mind. I went to college and nursing school, and learned so many things that have really benefited my life. I joined a Financial Services company and have learned a lot about how money works and why most people don't have any. (Hope that's not you.) I've also had to take many courses that didn't have anything to do with nursing or finances but were electives in the programs. Art history, for example, was great, and philosophy taught me a lot about human nature. All good input that can be stored in my computer. (Hope you have noticed that I use the words, 'Mind' and 'Computer' kind of interchangeably).

Put a mark beside this section as it is very important to understand this truth. Not only is our brain like a computer, it is also like a sponge. We know sponges will soak up liquids that they are placed into. Picture this now; squeeze the sponge first and then put it into the liquid. The absorption occurs much faster because of the negative pressure (or suction) that is created when you release the sponge. (*I should have raised the price of this book considering the tremendous amount of scientific knowledge I am sharing*). The brain is similar to that squeezed sponge. It is conditioned to absorb information.

The television, radio, magazine, and social media platforms have all really exploited that. Look at all the ads and commercials they expose us to. They are designed to get things into your mind. You would be amazed at how much companies are willing to pay for a 30 second commercial during the Superbowl for example. They want to get their products into your mind. By the time the first half is over, you want a pizza, beer, and a new truck. Go ahead and get the pizza and beer now but please read the rest of the book before you buy the truck.

Information can also be suggested very subtly through pop-ups and ads on the internet or in Social Media content. Remember the primary ports; the eyes and the ears. There are ads, short videos, and links to full infomercials, all designed to get information into your mind.

OK, I think we have covered this point enough. The key take-away is, look at the person that you want to be and the people that you want your children to turn out to be and control input into your computers accordingly. You can't control everything but control the things that you can.

Chapter 2

The Processor

Once we have things downloaded into our minds, they go through the Processor. Now of course, the things that we cover are not actually physically taking place and most of the times, the transfers take place subconsciously. There are places, however, where decisions must be made. I am sure you are aware that life is all about decisions. I cover the decision-making process very thoroughly in my book, 'Reincarnate Now!' Good decisions can make life's journey prosperous, whereas poor decisions can cause life altering events that produce regrets for years.

As input enters our minds, it goes through a system of processing and sorting. Things are sorted very differently from person to person. We may also process some things one way when we are young yet another way when we are a bit older. Let's take a look at the Processor and the Sorter.

We have already talked about our warning devices, Conscience and Conviction. Now we will discuss the elements of the processor. First, what does the processor do? It gathers all input from every source and determines if and where it fits in to the scheme of our lives. (This is really cool stuff, so don't leave me now.)

One of the components of the Processor contains is our lives Objectives. What are our lives' ambitions? What do we want for and out of life? We are going to use Bill as an example. Feel free to picture yourself as Bill as we see how the Processor works.

Bill here wants to be happy. He wants to be a good citizen, be successful, and be respected. (Please bear with the silly illustrations. I think they are funny, but it doesn't take much to amuse me.) Bill gets to work on a Monday morning and is approached by Nagging Nancy. "It's going to be another horrible Monday. I can't believe we have so much to do. Why don't they hire more help? Who made this coffee? It tastes like oil." Bill takes pride in his work ethics and loves his job. He sure doesn't need Nancy's negative vibes to start the day, so the Processor sends all of it to; you got it, the Trash Bin.

Neil passes by his office, looks in and says, "I'm going to work through lunch to make sure we are ready for the meeting this afternoon. I think we are good but just want to make sure. I'll be in the conference room if you want to join me." That's better. Bill is also very conscientious about his work. Positive energy flowing there and it is something that meets Bill's objectives, so it will be stored and acted upon.

Here he comes, Wacky Wayne. Wayne has a job there but never seems to work. All he does is roam about the halls looking for someone to talk to, or I should say gossip with. "Hey Bill, you working hard or hardly working? Ha Ha Ha! Boy that west wing is sure quiet. Heard the guy in payroll was hitting on the new mail girl and his assistant got mad and told his wife cause, well I think she had a ...." STOP. Bill and his Processor agreed to DELETE that entire thing. Definitely not beneficial intel.

On the way home, Bill turned on the radio and the news was filled with shootings, muggings, and other very disturbing items. He understands these things happen and he doesn't stick his head in the sand, but he is on his way home to his wife and children, and wants to be cheerful when he gets there; so the radio station is changed to some soft music and Bill sings along. The Processor says, 'We will do the news later'.

Before you start lecturing me on the realities of life, remember our mind is the best insulator that we have to keep the things around us from negatively affecting us. Yes, things may be bad at work and yes, horrible things happen every day in this world but dwelling on those things will not help us meet our objectives in life. It will only produce depression and anxiety; two things that will not be beneficial at all. There are times when unpleasant things should be processed but we can have control of when that is.

Secondly, the Processor operates within the guidelines of your Beliefs. Just a reminder, we are not all the same and neither are our beliefs. I would love to say that the distinction between right and wrong is a clear one, but it really does depend on the beliefs. When someone mentions beliefs, it is often associated with faith and religion. The truth is that it goes much further than that. We could spend several chapters just on this discussion alone, but I will try and keep it short.

We will just say that the things I believe in are processed through and filed for further use. The things that I do not believe in are rejected and sent to the trash bin, while the things that I am not sure about are sent to a file called, 'Needs Further Research'. In other words, I need to look at it more carefully before I decide whether or not I believe it. One quick example would be that of creative evolution. If someone were to say, "Everything we see evolved and there is no God," well, it would immediately be processed to the Trash Bin because I believe in God.

If someone were to say, "God created the universe and man, but over the course of centuries, some evolutionary processes have taken place." Now that is possible, doesn't conflict my belief in God, and needs some further research.

Some say, right is right and wrong is wrong, and there is no mixing of the two; you know, eye for an eye. Others say that there is no right and wrong, everything is relative; you know, situation ethics; it all depends on the situation. And there are many points in between these varied beliefs.

Thirdly, we have Morals in the Processor. (Hang tight; it may get a bit sticky here). Morals are supposed to keep us functioning within certain parameters in society. Unfortunately, there are so many things that are totally devoid of morality in this world today that the Processor works overtime just to keep that stuff out. I say today because things have gotten so much worse over the years. I have been around for 64 years and wow, what regression we have seen in ethics and morals. I look back twenty years and the difference between then and today, and then try to picture what things will be like twenty years from now. I shudder just thinking about it.

It is more important now than ever to let that processor hold on to your morals, beliefs, and objectives. But let's go back a bit further and answer this question. Where did you get your beliefs, morals, and objectives? There are several possibilities but most of the time they come from our upbringing. As a foundational point, they were derived from what our family believed and stood for and what we were taught by our parents. My father was the strong influential figure in our home and he believed in hard work, honesty, and helping those that had pressing needs. Interestingly enough, all three of his sons ended up working in the medical field.

Parenting is a very hard role as we are not just teachers and coaches in matters of life but also examples. One of the most damaging adages ever spoken is, "Do what I say, not what I do." I can vividly remember football practice, four of us pushing a sled around the field. Our 300-pound football coach (ah, not all muscle) would jump on it and say, "Come on ladies, it's about time you got into shape." We all thought the same thing but never said a word.

I really do believe that we develop a much better Processor within our children when we practice what we preach. Hey, we all make mistakes and slip but overall, what we say should be backed up by what we do. I can still hear a woman saying one time, "You kids better stop your (blankety blank) swearing. If I hear another (blank) cuss word I am gonna beat the (blank) out of you." Of course, she never did and today they all make sailors blush.

There is one more thing along this line, and that's the fact nothing ever works out 100%. I have seen children from divided homes or those raised by single Moms turn out to be successful and constructive members of society. I have also seen horror stories concerning people that grew up in really solid families where they were taught good morals and the parents lived clean and descent lives.

By the way, if you are wondering what on earth is going on with our world today, this would be a good place to start. The headlines I read make me sick sometimes and I can't help but wonder where the distinction between right and wrong is? More and more people seem to possess broken Processors.

As we mature (well, get older) our Processor begins to get tested. It now sees other sets of beliefs and morals. Peer pressure plays a big role in the drastic changes that occur in the lives of children. Some that had very sheltered childhoods soon find themselves exposed to so many other ways of looking at things. Experimentation begins and now that person reprograms the Processor to accept things that originally would have been discarded. But remember; we have control. That is the purpose for this book; to help us understand that even though there is so much out there that we will be exposed to, we are still in control of what we process into our minds and lives.

Our surroundings also play a huge part in what we are exposed to. Growing up in Still Hollow, Pennsylvania (population 100 or so counting cats and dogs) is quite different from growing up in the middle of a large city. I recently saw an article about a 12-year-old arrested for a gang related murder. It is so unfortunate that people have to live and children have to grow up living with the very things that make us shudder. Crime, drugs, gangs, and shootings are all common occurrences for these areas and CAN have a terrible effect on Processors. I said 'can' because it is not 'must'.

Many grow up in these areas sticking to their morals, ethics, and beliefs and refuse to process the nasty revolving world around them. Their resilience amazes me, and they certainly have earned my respect.

Make sure your Processor is functioning properly (Huge point here). If you are tempted to reprogram a bit, take the time to ask yourself, 'why' first. Why are you changing what you believe or what you stand for? The root question would be, '*Do you want your life to reflect your beliefs, ethics, and morals or are you changing those things because of how you found yourself living?*'

Just a couple of quick examples: Joe is now 51 years old. He has been in great shape all his life and has had virtually no health problems. He really believed good nutrition and exercise were vital to staying healthy. As he started aging, he noticed it was harder to keep the weight off and stick to even a modified exercise routine. He decided that he may have been too strict in the past and nutrition and exercise were probably over emphasized.

Instead of fighting a bit harder to keep his Processor on track, he reprogrammed it and now he doesn't exercise and eats what he wants. Guess what happened to Joe? (He started on my famous, 'Buy Bigger Clothes Diet.')

The church Barbara attends does not believe in divorce and she was also strongly against it; until her husband became the WORSE version of the famous marital vow 'for better for worse'; and she met Bill. Now she thinks divorce is OK in *some* circumstances (including hers).

It is sad to think that so many children are raised by their parents to believe in God only to go off to some college and be taught atheistic views from those that hold education as their god. In just one semester, they abandon the foundational convictions their parents taught them to follow abstract theories.

You can think of other examples as well I am sure. Now on the other hand, I never really got involved in politics. I hated reading about it, discussing it, and certainly getting into debates about it. But I didn't actually trash it all; I put it in the 'Needs Further Research' file and after doing some due diligence on the matter, I have changed my beliefs. I am now a very vocal, outspoken, opinionated, and an active participant in politics. I feel I was wrong in the past and it is my duty to get and stay informed and spread what I feel is the truth about what matters in our country. (Wait till you see my next book). So reprogramming is not always bad; but please ask WHY?

Recap

Just a quick recap before we move on to the Sorter.

- Our eyes and our ears are the most important ports into our minds. We can't control everything that goes into our minds but what we can control, we should.
- We have a couple of warning mechanisms that alarm when we are exposed to things we do not want into our minds; Conscience and Conviction.

- Once into our minds, the Processor decides whether it goes into the Trash Bin or sent on in for further sorting.
- The Processor is governed by what we believe, what we stand for and what our life's objectives are.
- A lot of the Processor's elements are formed in childhood but are later affected by our environment and peer pressure.
- Processors can be reprogrammed to allow more or less into the sorting center. Changes should be thoroughly questioned to ensure it is being done for the right reasons.

Chapter 3

❖❖❖❖❖

Sorting

These next two chapters are really where the rubber meets the road. This is where data is sorted and placed into appropriate files. In this chapter, we will discuss some general things about sorting. The next chapter will highlight several folders that the information goes into. The important thing to remember is that **this is where you have the most control.** From the files, actions are taken, your life is lived, and the results follow. Wrong folder, wrong action, guess what; bad result.

Just as the Processor has elements, so does the Sorter. There are things that will influence which folder is chosen for items that are sorted.

Self-esteem is one of the biggies, and in my opinion it is one reason why so many people don't ever reach their fullest potential in life. Even though self-esteem is what one thinks of *themselves*, it is often formed by *outside* sources. Hollywood has created an image in so many female minds that if they don't have perfect hair and perfect teeth and weigh just above a skeleton, they can't be successful in life. Men have to have perfect faces, nice hair or bulging muscles. If you don't believe me, look and see how much the average American spends on fitness and beauty products. It will blow your mind.

I can tell you for a fact as will anyone that studied successful people, the qualities that matter come from the inside of a person, not from outward appearances. I cringe when I hear about young women suffering and dying from eating disorders because they want to look thin. Not all of the women affected by these disorders are ill because of the image issues but thousands are. And I want to tell you a little secret. Ready? When you get older, unless you can afford multiple plastic surgeries like the Hollywood gang, you aren't gonna turn too many heads; **but what you have on the inside will keep you just as desirable as ever.**

Education is another area where your self-esteem can be shattered. It seems that the more degrees you have the more respected you are. Now, I am certainly an advocate of higher education. Where would we be without the professionals in our lives that possess higher degrees like doctors, scientists, and others? I once had to have an open-heart surgery several years ago and I am certainly glad that the person who did it had more than a GED.

What I am saying in essence is that a person can certainly be successful in many ways without a lot of degrees. PLEASE do not get me wrong. I believe you should get all the education you can to work toward the goal of being whatever you want to be; just don't sell yourself short if you aren't highly educated. You can still be a giant!

I could show you quite a list of successful people that didn't have higher education and some that didn't even finish high school. Perhaps, you have heard of John Rockefeller, Henry Ford, Dave Thomas (founder of Wendys; just got a craving for a nice cup of chili), and ah, what was his name, oh ya, Abraham Lincoln.

The point is, as things process through your mind,

don't discard them because of low self-esteem. 'I CAN' is a very powerful phrase. Watch me convince myself of something.

"What do you really want to be in life?"

"I want to be a doctor, but I CAN'T because I didn't go to medical school."

"Go to medical school then."

"I can't because I haven't been to college."

"Go to college then."

"Well I …. Well I…. hey, I CAN".

You CAN do whatever you put your mind and heart into. I have been around for 64 years and I've encountered so many successful and unsuccessful people in the course of my life's journey. In the vast majority of cases, desire, dedication and hard WORK trumps out many other characteristics including a pretty face and bulging biceps. (I am not saying that I do not have bulging biceps. I do not have a pretty face).

A second element of the Sorter is what I call Capacity. Now I know you are wondering, "Wow, is he gonna hit on the not so bright folks here?" Well, the answer is of course not. There is a huge difference between intelligence and capacity. I am sure you have heard the term, 'narrow minded', sometime in your life. And the opposite is then open minded. Narrow minded people are reluctant to take in additional input, whereas open minded people are more willing to. My way of reconciling them is summed up in two phrases; be narrow minded with some flexibility or be open minded with some parameters. That puts the two pretty close together. Basically, you don't want to gullibly accept everything that comes along, neither do you want to close yourself off to new information. Balance is the key word here.

The function of the Sorter is huge, so you need to be involved in sorting. You say, "Well, it's my mind so how can I not be in control of the sorting?" Glad you asked. Subconsciously, our minds do so many things that we do not make a decision on. In my other book that I mentioned earlier, I spent a lot of time talking about a term I call 'Conscious Awareness'. It means being consciously aware of what we are doing and what we are deciding. So many activities in our everyday life are on what I call, 'Autopilot'. For example, I don't have to think and decide to brush my teeth, it's on Autopilot. The same thing often occurs when we receive information. The sorting is almost automatic without thought.

Here's Ted. He is 53 years old and in fairly good health. He is watching TV and a blurb comes on about Colon Cancer screening. At this point, Ted doesn't give the thought the time of day and files it in the, 'Not Important', file in his mind. A couple of weeks later, he is waiting for his Dad in the Doctor's office and the TV in there keeps displaying medical information. The slides he saw were showing the number of people that die each year from Colon Cancer, how it seldom has symptoms in early stages, and the fact that early detection saves thousands of lives. Guess what, Ted pulled it out of the 'Not Important' file and placed into his, 'Take Action' file. Why? Because he was now consciously making a decision.

The process of Sorting also has a lot to do with your personality. I am going to use the person I know most about to make an illustration; me. First of all, I am a fairly open-minded person, so I entertain many things before I file them in the trash. If I get a telemarketer call for an extended warranty on my car, I dismiss it because I have already decided that I don't want it. If it is for a business opportunity, I generally listen and often request more information.

Sometimes, I do buy things that are advertised on TV. There are some neat things and most of the time, I was very satisfied with my purchase. (Some of these new glues really work; my thumb and index finger are now one big finger).

I am also a softy. (Please don't tell anyone). My heart breaks when I watch St. Jude Hospital commercials and yes, I donate regularly. The animal shelter commercials and cruelty to animal rescue efforts do as well. I haven't seen one for a while now but remember the CARE commercials? Talk about heart wrenching stuff. I can name several charities that I feel are worthy and that I regularly donate to. However, reeling it in a bit, you and I both know that you cannot donate to everything you come across. I had to make some decisions. The point is because I am a bit open minded and soft hearted, I do a lot more conscious decision making than many others.

I know some people that never buy anything they see advertised on TV, don't donate to anything, and immediately hang up on all telemarketers. I think most people are somewhere in between them and me.

Chapter 4

The Folders

Important – Not Important

Just like on a computer, to stay organized and focused, we have to place things into various folders. Now let's take a look at some of the folders that we place things into. These will be contrasting folders. For proper filing into these, conscious decision making is necessary.

Now back to Ted. Why was the Colon Cancer screening dismissed at first and then later acted upon? Because first, it was deemed not important but later it was reclassified as being important. That brings us to another truth to garnish on Sorting. We need to have clear values on what is important. I am going to make one huge statement here that can literally change your life. Ready? *The earlier in life we start recognizing the importance of things the better off we will be.* Delaying this process can be, and often is devastating. How about some of these?

"I'll start worrying about my health when I get old. I am feeling fine now."

"I'll start saving for retirement when I hit 45 or so. I need the money for other things now."

"I'll have the talk with my son about drugs in a few years. He is only 12."

Wow! Do I even have to comment here? I will spare the commentary as I am sure you get the point. As we move on, you may want to take a look and see if you need to re-think some things you are currently classifying as unimportant. Your life, your health, your happiness, and your future, depends on what you NOW deem as important.

Let's look at another qualification of what makes something important by asking this question; 'Important to who?' Most human beings don't just care about themselves but also about others. As we are deciding what is important, we need to think about that very fact. We should always be looking to see if there is someone else that it may be important to.

Bill (Ted is getting his Colon Cancer screening done) is working when 5 PM rolls around. He has a huge presentation set for the next morning and he is already exhausted. He is about to call his wife to tell her that he is going to work late on the presentation when he remembers his son has his first baseball game at 6 PM. Almost without thinking, he tells himself that the presentation is very important and he can catch his son's next game. That's basically saying that the game is not important. Back to the question; not important to WHO? It may not be very important to him considering the circumstances but to his wife and his son…. his first baseball game…..HUGE!

It is mid-August and Bill has still not put in for a family vacation. He is a work-aholic and could go all year without one. Vacations are just not important. Ah, to WHO? His wife has also worked very hard at her job all year and families need that special time together. It is really important; I think you get the idea. When you are deciding on what is and what is not important, also consider the ones you care about.

One last thought on what is important. So many times we cocoon ourselves in a very tiny place. We do not want to be concerned about what is going on outside our cocoon. We just don't want to get involved with things that do not seem to directly affect us.

Thank God back in colonial days, there were those that saw the need for our country to become an independent nation. Men and women took a stand and fought a great battle in order for our nation to be born. The visionaries who saw a nation where people could have freedom and liberty set the pace and raised their voices against oppression and tyranny.

Although the Declaration of Independence was ratified by the 13 colonies, not everyone was on board. Some continued to side with the British, (Loyalists) and many, others sat idly by to see what was going to happen. It wasn't their fight…. or was it. After it was over, they sure enjoyed the new nation so why not get involved? Why not stand alongside those that fought? Why not throw a little tea in the Harbor? (OK, went a little too far there).

We should be constantly thinking about the most important things in life like our children's education, our communities, our churches, our country, and more. Just a note, we just elected a new president. (No comment in this book.) How many eligible voters are there in America? And how many actually voted? Are all these things important? Well, they certainly are, so put them in the important folder and get involved.

Want – Need

You may be tempted to pass up this section but please don't. How many times have we made poor decisions because we placed things in the wrong one of these two folders? The most common error made here is wanting something so badly that you convince yourself that you actually need it. The real problem that occurs is that when you deem something as a need instead of just a want, you end up doing it. This will often take time, money and resources away from other things that you may truly need.

Here is Neil. (Ted is still having his Colon Screening and Bill is at his son's baseball game. See, they got something out of this book). Neil's car is 5 years old with 80,000 miles on it. It is in good condition and really doesn't have anything wrong with it. He was just thinking on his way home from work what a good car it has been.

He looked in the neighbor's driveway and saw a brand-new car. It was gorgeous. He snooped around a while until his neighbor came out and showed it off a bit. Wow, what a nice car! Then the hook came. His neighbor told him that the dealer he went to was a friend of his and could get him a good deal.

Guess what, Neil now WANTS a new car. He began thinking of how cool it would be to have one. That look, that smell, and all those new added features like the camera for backing up and defrosters on the mirrors drove his want even further. A new car would certainly look nice in his driveway.

Yep, you took the words right out of my mouth. Neil started re-thinking. "Well, my car does have 80,000 miles on it, and it is paid off. The A/C probably needs recharged, the headlights are getting cloudy, and it will be time for new tires soon." You guessed it. Neil now NEEDS a new car. You are probably smiling as this has probably been you with something or another.

Here is the other side of the story. The last time Neil had his Heat Pump serviced, the technician told him it was an old unit and was wearing out. It would need to be replaced soon, and that would be about $6000. He had been putting what his car payment had been into savings so that when the heat pump did go out, he would have the funds to replace it. (Excellent thinking by the way). If Neil, who NEEDS a new car gets it with a nice sized car payment, he won't be able to put any more money aside for his new heat pump which I think you will agree, would be a need.

We will visit with Neil again shortly. Just remember, we often sacrifice resources, time, and money from things that we need in order to get the things that we want. Think it through.

Sally has always wanted to be a nurse. She started and finished nursing school and state boards are next. She is absolutely petrified of exams. While in nursing school, she worked part time at one of the fancier restaurants in town. As she was completing her program in school, they offered her a big promotion into fulltime management. She didn't mind the work and was honored to get the promotion, but she still desperately wanted to be a nurse. Because of her fear of taking the exam, she decided to work fulltime at the restaurant and study a bit until she felt ready to take her exam. (Dragging this out a bit I know but hang on, there is a point here).

Basically, she needs to take the exam to achieve her dream of being a nurse. She wants to work fulltime to make more money and avoid the exam, also to take time away from a need to spend on a want.

Many things come down to these two folders, and choosing appropriately makes the difference between success and failure. Some are big things like Sally's exam and others not so seemingly significant.

- Mary needs to save money but wants to shop all the time.
- Gary needs to exercise but wants to watch TV.
- Terry needs to lose weight but wants that pie and ice cream.
- That athlete needs to train but wants to hang out with his friends.

I think you get the point. There is a difference between a need and a want.

Sometimes you want something so badly that you convince yourself you need it. Don't take away from the things you need in order to get the things you want.

Now – Later

That brings us to the next pair of folders; Now and Later. Oh boy is this ever gonna be fun. Back to the baby in the crib that needs a bottle or changed or just wants attention. WHAAAAA! When the mother hears that she says "Be there in a couple of minutes." The baby stops crying and says, "OK." Well, probably not. We are programmed from infancy that when we want something, we want it NOW.

Things you can seldom get away with when dealing with children.

- We'll eat when we get home.
- We'll stop at the next rest area.
- You can go out and play when the grass dries.
- I'll get you that for your birthday.
- We'll fly the drone later this afternoon.

Those of you that are parents know exactly what I am talking about and most of us can even remember being guilty of that when we were kids. There is just something about human nature that doesn't like waiting; now is much better. Somehow, we translate 'later', as 'never.' "We're never going to get there. You're never going to get that for me." They say that patience is a virtue, so I am assuming that most of us aren't very virtuous. (I know I wasn't till I read this book.) (*Advertising at it's best.*)

Now, just before Neil drives down to the dealership to get that new car that he ah, needs, he stops and thinks about the whole situation. After arguing with himself for a moment, he came to this conclusion. I want a new car, but I do not really need a new car right now. When that heat pump goes out, I will need it replaced right away. He comes up with a grand idea. I will get what I need now and get what I want later.

He already had $3000 saved. If he would just put away $300 a month, in 10 months he had his $6000 for the heat pump. He even waited a few months longer and saved up $1200 for a down payment on his new car. Great job Neil. First, he made the decision that the new car was indeed a want and not a need, even though he could have still gotten the car because he wanted it. (We all know that happens). He decided to put his want in the later folder ensuring he had allocated money for the heat pump FIRST. We would save ourselves a lot of heartbreak if we would put things in the proper folders.

Now Cliff was working in the yard and had some tightness in his chest. He's only 38 and has been healthy all of his life. He saw his doctor who recommended a full cardiac workup. His finances and insurance are not the best and he will be looking at going in debt to have the workup done. Let's see how you would handle this. Is the workup something that he really needs? I heard you say yes and you are correct. Should he do it now and go in debt or wait till later when his finances are better?

Before you answer, think about this. Should he suffer a heart attack, even if he lives, he will be out of work for a while and have a great deal more expense and what a tragedy if it would be worse. So you are right again. It's a no brainer; NOW it is! Now and later are two folders that we should consciously get correct. It is not always easy to decide and many times we have to think about short and long term effects on where we place things.

Fast – Slow

Now, what on earth do I mean by separating things

into fast and slow? I think you will quickly see where I am going here but wow, you could come up with so many illustrations of why you need to get this right. I will start out with a personal example, so you get the picture.

When I was in high school, I ran a lot. I loved jogging and just enjoyed the solitude and the scenery. It was really therapeutic. Now, I miss it so badly due to a bum knee and bad heart. I once told my Doctor that I would love to go on one last run. He said if you do, it will probably be your one last run. (So, I walk)

Back to the story. My friend was a runner on the school track team. He knew I ran a lot and asked me if I wanted to enter a race with him in Pittsburgh. It was a 660-yard event. Now remember, I ran long distances but slowly. This was a short fast race.

I was so nervous as we drove down to the race. In my heat, I was on the outside lane and with staggered starts, I was way ahead on the other runners. As you know, when running a circular track, the ones in the inner lanes catch up. When the gun sounded, I took off like a shot and was running as fast as I could. After about 10 seconds, there was no one catching up to me; I was still way ahead. In about 10 more seconds, someone turned my air off, turned my legs into rubber and handed me a 500 lb. backpack. That's what it felt like anyhow.

After my near collapse and the race was over, my friend came over to me and said, "What on earth were you doing? You sprinted flat out for the first lap. You can't do that for a 660-yard race. You have to pace yourself." "Ah ya, right…. Thanks so much. I didn't think about that." The morale of the story is that some things require that fast sprint but for others, you better pace yourselves.

Now we are going to review just a bit through the various sorting processes. Let's pick a subject that is something I am very familiar with but hate; dieting. I'll ask and you answer.

Is the subject of dieting a thing that we would let into our minds? Yes, you are correct! Is it important? Yes, again. Is it a want or need? Could be either, but most likely it would be a need. Is it something we should do now or later? If it is for health reasons, now would be the time. OK, last question; is it something we want to do fast or slow? In order to answer that question, let's take a look at a few things.

- Is it really safe to lose 20 pounds in 2 weeks?
- Would losing weight really quickly be considered a crash diet or a lifestyle change?
- Is the end goal to lose as much as possible and as fast as possible with the probability of gaining it back or losing it and keeping it off?
- How many crash dieters do you think put the weight back on if they do NOT make any permanent dietary and lifestyle changes?

So, I think we have come to a conclusion here, dieting should be paced safely as to allow for adequate nutrition and needed lifestyle changes. Fast, crash diets seldom work.

Let's take a look at Ted. (Colon was OK. Thanks for asking.) Ted is a mechanic and after much thought, decided to leave his job and open his own shop. On the opening day, he had some friends come by and he had a few other customers as well. He set some goals, (we will discuss that in a bit,) and began tracking them. He set his goal profit level at $5000 a month by the end of month 3, $6,000 by the end of month 6, and $7,000 a month by the end of his first year.

He practically worked non-stop without hiring another mechanic to decrease expenses, invested in some marketing materials, and begged family and friends to tell others about his shop. Those of you that know a thing about business knows that Ted here is going way too fast. One of the first things he should have done was to place this in a slow category, realizing that it takes TIME and patience to get any business going.

Do you know why 45% of all new businesses fail within the first five years? The same reason that I came in last in that race. (Oh, I didn't mention that, did I?) I sprinted instead of pacing myself. This is different than the 'now' and 'later' folders.

If you are a younger person, please do not get angry with this next section. I am not talking about you but other young people. (Snicker, snicker) It seems like this generation (Generation Z) and the one before it (Millennials) have really packed their Slow folder. I have heard them boast on how they squeezed their four years of college into eight years. They wanted to take a couple of years off after high school before rushing into a career or college, take a break between each semester, and other things that really slowed their progression. After all, they can always move back in with Mom and Dad, (and they do). Sometimes, fast is good. Get that degree or get that job and get going with your life.

Do you remember how we sprinted to get our driver's license, to get accepted into college, to get that first job and car, and get out on our own? Not so much nowadays. So how do we determine whether or not we go fast or slow? It all boils down to our goals. Goal setting, both short and long term, is a major ingredient to success. Here are two key points to remember.

- If you are in a **sprint towards a long-term goal,** it will be very easy to get discouraged. Ted, trying to reach his long-term financial goal for his garage in just one year could make him begin to doubt his decision. He just needed to align his goals with an appropriate timeline. Trying to lose too much weight too quickly would produce the same problem. Achieving short-term goals on the way to your long-term goal is the ticket.
- If you **take too long to reach goals**, apathy will soon set in and you may find yourself becoming stagnant. Procrastination is a huge weapon that failure uses to defeat all of us that are poised toward achieving our goals. When the light is green, go.

NOTE: There is no shame in not being able to set timelines for various goals, not to mention the fact that we are all different. Use all the resources that are available to you in properly handling this step. I do not know what a good weight loss timeline would look like for ME. My Doctor's office can help as can various accepted articles and journals on the internet. I do know that weight loss is generally slower for those that have less to lose. (OK no more medical advice here).

How long will it take to get this business going? Ask for some input from others that have been there, and again, search the internet for some information that can help you to set those timelines. As always, it would be wise to do all this research before you jump into your endeavor. Also, be flexible and make adjustments for unexpected events and circumstances.

One last example: when I was in growing up, my mother used to fix potatoes and eggs. Basically, it is a mixture of fried potatoes and scrambled eggs. (Making you hungry?) Pretty simple right? I got home late one evening from football practice and my parents were away. I decided that I wanted potatoes and eggs. So, I cut the potatoes and put them in the skillet, and then added 3 eggs that I scrambled in a bowl. I fried the concoction and what a horrible meal it was. (To this day, I cannot eat potatoes and eggs.) You ladies are probably smiling; I think so. Yep, the potatoes were not done so I kept turning the heat up and frying them. And that of course burned the eggs. So, I ended up having undercooked potatoes and burned eggs. YUCK!

When Betty Crocker (Mom) got home, I didn't have to tell her that I had some issues with supper as she could smell it and saw the pan. She then informed me that she always fried the potatoes slowly until they were done before adding the eggs and just fried them for a minute.

Makes perfect sense now…. there are some things you have to cook slower.

Relationships – Associations

Please read this section very carefully as I do not want you to get the wrong impression on some of the things we cover. A great deal of life is centered around the interactions that we have with other people. Often times as we interact, we need to decide if the people we are interacting with should develop into relationships or remain as just associations or acquaintances. Much of the decision making here will seem to center around judging or making judgements. Please understand the fact that we should not judge **people** but we do have to judge what **effects** those people have on us.

Take for example; do you remember nagging Nancy? Everything she says is dripping with negativity. Her glass is half empty (or more) and there is never anything good going on in the world. I am sure you have met people like that. I do NOT judge her and say, "Nancy is a terrible person." But I do make judgements on what continuous contact with her does to me. It brings me down and eats away at my positivity. So, Nancy is not in my inner circle and yes, she remains just an association.

BUT just because we have that type of association doesn't mean that if she ever had a need, I wouldn't be there for her. That is what we humans do. We help those in need regardless of what type of relationship we have with them.

Most of the time when it comes to people, we initially only see the cover. One of the problems our world has today comes from 'Cover Judgements.' We have just a brief encounter with someone and we start judging them immediately. This book, for example, I am over halfway through and I don't have a title for it yet. I do hope you are getting some valuable things out of it, but unless I come up with a catchy Title and Subtitle with a cool cover, it probably won't sell.

I am not now nor ever will be in the people judging business. I do make judgments on what they say and what they do. I have to because I need to decide where I place them in my life.

I do not drink much, so as a result I do not hang out with party animals. I don't think they are terrible people I just don't have a connection with them; that's all. I am not into drugs, so I avoid that crowd. I am very goal oriented so I do find myself gravitating to those that can impart helpful wisdom and experiences. I feel I live a pretty clean life, so now you can see the reason I choose people with good morals and ethics to be friends with. I do not feel that I am better than anyone else. I am not part of the upper crust that looks at others like crumbs. But I do feel, however, that I have to choose my close relationships very carefully.

Be honest; how many times have you heard this; "So and so was such a good boy but then he started hanging out with the wrong crowd and now, bless his heart, he….." I believe with all my heart that this lesson ought to be taught countless times to our children. Children are impressionable, yield to peer pressure and have an overwhelming desire to be accepted. Believe me, there are a lot of people that will accept them but they won't be the right type of people.

One more note here; we get tremendously busy with our lives. Don't forget those that you do have relationships with. Don't let them slip down to associations; and yes this includes FAMILY. I sure hope you are not someone that sits at home evening after evening wondering when you are going to hear from your grown children, when you are going to spend some time with those grandchildren, and when you are going to hear from your sister or brother. And I certainly hope you are not someone that has gotten so busy with 'life' that you made the family that you grew up with a mere association.

Time is a key ingredient in relationships. You have no idea how much phone calls, text messages, and visits to a loved one or a dear friend means to them. (Or perhaps you do). Nothing new that we have in our lives now should replace the dear relationships that we have with family and friends. (Starting to get a bit teary eyed here so I better move on. This is real life stuff we are talking about). I'll say it but you may also be thinking it, "What I would give to be close to _____ again."

Several years ago, I was with a church group that visited nursing homes. We really enjoyed singing, talking, and just spending time with the folks there. We were often told that we were the only company they ever had. I cannot tell you how many of them told us they wished that some of their family members would visit them once and a while. Can you imagine just how much a little time could brighten up their lives?

Hey! Want to have some fun. Put the book down for a minute and get your phone out and start calling; family and friends, those that you have seen recently;

some perhaps not so recently; some years ago. Call and see how they are doing. Tell them you miss them, arrange some visits, ask them what they are up to, and tell them about a great little book you are reading. (Sorry, couldn't help myself). After that, get your address book out and do the same. Send some cards, texts, and just rekindle some of those relationships. You will be amazed what it will do for them and you as well.

Wrapping this up; don't be quick to judge people but be a good judge of what they say and do, and then decide the folder they should go into. I promise you that if you can teach your children this principle, it will save you and them a lot of trouble and heartache. I can vouch for that from experience.

Conscious – Subconscious

If you get a chance to read my book, 'Reincarnate Now!' Please do so because it covers this topic in much more detail. You know as well as I do that sometimes we do things intentionally by being consciously aware of what we are doing. Other times, we do things subconsciously with very little or no thinking involved. Let me make a few statements here that are vitally important.

- We should subconsciously or automatically do as many good things as we can, basically forming GOOD HABITS. Get into a habit of exercising, eating right, reading good books, (I was going to say "Like this one" but I didn't) brushing your teeth, and others. Once they become habits, the chance that we will do them regularly is much higher.

- We should stop as many bad things as we can that we do subconsciously. Smokers don't say, "OK I am making a decision to have a cigarette." They just do it routinely, especially at their golden times such as after meals, in the morning, and before they go to bed. Others are snackers and grazers, munching all day long on the wrong types of food. Very bad for weight and cholesterol. They don't decide to do it, it's just a BAD HABIT.

- We should be constantly examining the things that we do subconsciously. Many times you will see that you do so many things so routinely that you don't realize you are doing them. Here's just one example of something that I caught myself doing. I have been dieting for long time. Not a crash diet but limiting snacks and portion control. I also do most of the cooking and help with cleaning up afterwards. I never realized it but when I cook, I munch. When I clean up, I munch. I watch my portions during meals to keep the calorie count down, but then I munch. I don't get up from the table and decide, "OK, now I will finish this up because there is just a little left, and grab a cookie because they are sitting beside the sink, I just do it."

- Lastly, it takes time to form and break habits, so be patient. Whatever it is, we need to consciously do it over and over again until it becomes a habit or a subconscious action. Get a house with a fenced in back yard and watch that dog walk inside that perimeter over and over again. The first day or so, you don't see anything but give it a few weeks and there will be a nice dirt track formed around the yard. Why? Because the walking was done repeatedly. Create some good tracks in your life.

Summing it up, think about this; the more decisions we have to make the more possibilities there are that we will make a poor decision. Make good and deliberate decisions, perform it so routinely that it becomes a habit and you are set. I'll give you two more quick personal examples.

In the past, I was not a regular seatbelt wearer. It was strange because as an emergency responder, I have been to so many vehicle accident fatalities where the victims were not wearing seatbelts. Anyhow, when they made it law that you had to wear your seatbelts, I started buckling up. I had to remind myself for quite some time. Now it is just so automatic I don't even think about it.

Most of the time, I back out of my driveway. When I make the turn to go, I would put the car into 'Drive' before the car had completely stopped. One day my other half, who is an "excellent" back seat driver, told me she heard that what I was doing was hard on the transmission. This time her criticism of my driving was right. (rare occasion). For a while, I said to myself, "reverse, STOP, drive." Now it is automatic. I think you see how important that subconscious folder really is.

Trust – Doubt

Here are two good folders to look at. We really do need to spend some time when deciding which folder that the received information goes into. Let's start with people. When it comes to people;

- I can trust them because I know them well enough to know they are being truthful. There are those that I have known for a while that aren't exactly straight shooters. They are not in my trust folder.

- I can trust some people because of the positions they are in, leaving me with no reason to doubt them, like my Doctors.

- I can trust some because I have seen a track record of honesty and integrity. If I have been dealing with someone for a while and they have always been honest with them, I feel I can trust them.

- I have a real hard time trusting those that have been dishonest in the past. I know, we are supposed to forgive and forget but I am always cautious in this situation.

- I am usually skeptical of those I do not know that have agendas. I was debating on some furniture one time and asked the salesman how long the 'special' sale was on. He looked at his watch and said, "Till noon." What furniture store stops a sale at noon? So I politely said, "Goodbye." If I can't trust him on the length of the sale, I am surely not going to trust him on the quality of the furniture.

Now there is a middle area outside of these folders that is meant for information that needs further review. Just because someone has been dishonest with you doesn't mean they are always dishonest. On the other side, I sometimes check out the information a bit more thoroughly of those honest people that I don't know well.

We also have to consider the ramifications (I try to get at least a couple big, sophisticated words in each book) of what they are telling us. If Cliff tells me he caught a 32 inch bass, my life will not depend on the accuracy of his measurement. If he tells me that I could be a millionaire in a year with just a $20,000 investment; ah, gonna check that one out very well.

I will have another book coming out soon that will discuss this in detail, but I have some bad news about the news; it can be very slanted. I am not going into detail here, but I just want to say that you should do your own personal research before believing everything that you hear or read in the news. Now, if it is an event like a fire in California or a shooting or hurricane that is a different matter altogether. But when you read or hear things of a political nature, please tread cautiously on the trust side. If you don't believe me, watch different news stations and you will get conflicting commentary on the information. I think the polls on this last election will prove that point.

Here is another thing I want to share with you. As I mentioned earlier, I personally do not mind telemarketers. Some have good products and that is one way to market them. It does get annoying sometimes when you get the same call over and over again.

I have a slightly different opinion on professional scammers, people that prey on the gullibility and lack of understanding of others. Those that have no problem stealing from the elderly that have next to nothing anyhow. Here it is…. I think you are totally disgusting and need to find an honest job. (And I hope someone scams you someday of everything you have).

My other half keeps getting calls from the 'Social Security Department' telling her she owes them thousands of dollars but if she would call them back, they can arrange a settlement. Please believe me, collections from government agencies, creditors, and banks will be accompanied by official WRITTEN notifications on official letterhead. Don't listen to them, instead just tell them to mail you the details. That usually ends it right there because if it is a scam, you will never see anything.

I could go on and on discussing TV ads, advertisements, and more but just a takeaway here. Be cautious of unreliable sources and people, and do some research before taking any action. Don't put it into your trust folder until you fully investigate and are sure you can trust the information. And don't lose sleep on the size of Cliff's fish. (Does sound kind of fishy though because two days ago it was 27 inches.) ah, fishermen.

Self – Others

I think we all know that we are born with instincts that are based on necessities such as food, water, shelter, and safety. I can remember as my children were growing, they reached a certain age when everything was, "MINE."

They might not actually want it, but they sure didn't want anyone else having it either. As we get older, that starts to dissipate a bit and we are a bit more considerate of the needs and wants of others.

As we mature, most people will have a dominant force concerning these two folders. Some strengthen the inner 'Me' and some become more aware of what they can do for 'others'.

I have been in the medical field for 46 years. I have loved being in a field that allows me to help others. I am a Registered Nurse and really believe that medical professionals answer a calling to care for other people. It is natural for parents to care for their children, and natural for all of us to care for those that we love. Caring for total strangers takes a bit more.

I have to say that I have seen a vast difference in the medical and nursing fields over the past decade or so. I have interviewed hundreds of people for various positions. A question that I asked frequently had to do with their reason for getting into the medical field. Shockingly, many in recent years said they lost their job in another vocation and heard that the medical field was a growing and steady opportunity. And there is nothing wrong with that as long as they develop that nurturing care for patients. However, it is so unfortunate that many do not, and it is pretty easy to identify those in it for just the paycheck.

We all only have so many hours in each week and if you are like me, we sure can fill each one up. Bill could have spent all his time on his job (me) but he realized how important baseball games and vacations were to his family, (others). Do you see all the volunteers in the hospital? They are giving their time for others. Do you see those that run soup kitchens, food drives, and become Big Brothers? They are all giving of a very valuable commodity … time. It means a lot to them being able to help others and you can't even estimate how much it means to those they are serving.

I have never been and never will be rich. But you know what? I feel rich when I send in my checks to St. Jude Hospital, and the Shriners, and Easter Seals, and the Disabled American Veterans and others. I can't give each one a lot but I give what I can. I have seen how much some wealthy people donate and my hat goes off to them. Donations do so much for sick children, those injured in the line of duty, those with cancer and so on. Many organizations could not exist without the financial help they get from donors. I am sure that many of you are like me and just get ill watching some of the commercials of those in need. Don't ever lose that tug on your soul.

Others seem to feel quite OK looking out for numero uno … themselves. I do not condemn or judge them but I just have problems being around terribly selfish people. How many 60 – 70 year old pastors cut the church lawn and clean the church with his wife while their church members hunt, fish, shop, golf or just relax? How many elderly people live around us or are we related to that could use some help around the house and yard or could use a ride to the store to get some groceries?

I am not boasting here but I have to share this as it made me feel like a billionaire. I was in line at a food store one day and the lady in front of me had a baby and a toddler. As they were ringing up her groceries, I was on the phone but then noticed she was going through the things that were already rung up. She had to take a couple cans of soup, a box of cereal, and one carton of formula back because she didn't have enough money.

I didn't look in her direction as I am sure she was embarrassed. She left the store with her other groceries and the bag boy was gathering the other items to put back on the shelf. I told them to quickly ring them up with my stuff and run them out to her. It was only a few bucks but when the bag boy got to her and told her what happened, she bowed and shook her head. I did not cry, I repeat, I did not cry, (but almost, well sorta) anyhow I hadn't felt so good in a long time. Spend some time seeing all that you can put in the 'Others" folder.

Chapter 5

Accessories

Okay, so now that the information in our computers (minds), has been processed and some was sorted into various folders, let's take a look at a few of the accessories that our mind develops as well. These develop through the things that we learn and experience.

Caution

We can receive different types of caution messages. Perhaps, it's a spam caution or a caution that we are entering a site that could be harmful. This accessory is a very important one and should not be ignored. Let's take a look at a few examples.

Driving down the road one day, you get a text that says, "You are not going to believe what Terry just posted on Facebook." You smile with anticipation and start your attempt to open Facebook on your phone …. while driving! It takes a bit more attention that you first realize and suddenly you hear a horn blowing and sure enough, you noticed that you have drifted into the oncoming lane. You are able to get back in time, thank goodness, but it was close. That was some *experience*. The next day you are driving again, and you were trying to get to your office before a conference call started but you were delayed at your last stop; no problem, you can still dial in. You start to look at your calendar for the call-in number and suddenly a CAUTION flashes through your mind telling you that you almost hit an oncoming car yesterday by fiddling with your phone. It was too close to repeat so you find a safe place to pull over and dial into the call. A past experience produced a caution and trouble was averted.

How many accidents are caused by this very same scenario? So many because the caution was ignored. What about the ones that have not had that experience? The same caution should come from the *knowledge* that driving requires our full attention and we should be consciously aware of what we are doing. Distractions like fooling with phones, radios, screaming kids in the back seat, and others have caused many accidents and fatalities. Now, I can almost assure you that caution signal will be more noticeable the next time you are tempted to be distracted while driving because of this information. Please don't test it but watch. You will say, "Wow, he was right."

Andy is trying to save the cost of hiring an electrician, so he decides to add an electrical outlet in the basement himself. He has all the supplies he needs and starts the process. Now he *knows* what could happen if he touches the wiring incorrectly but he is not sure which breaker to turn off, he doesn't want to turn all the electricity off, and besides, he is in a hurry. As he begins, that CAUTION flashes in his mind. "I could blow a fuse, start a fire, get electrocuted; perhaps I should try and find the breaker for this circuit." Good thinking Andy.

The next Saturday, Andy decides to replace a leaking water line. (Why doesn't he just go golfing?) He will have to turn the water off, undo several connections that are a bit corroded, and replace them. He has all the materials and is ready to get started. Guess what happens? Yep, the CAUTION flashes in his mind. If something goes wrong, he would have to go without water or call a plumber for a very expensive, emergency house call, so he decides to proceed. In an attempt to loosen a fitting because it was so corroded, it broke the line. He goes back to the fitting behind it and he can't even budge that one. You guessed it; the plumber arrived a couple hours later, fixed the lines, and handed Andy a very expensive bill. Now Andy will have a much stronger caution the next time this scenario arises, knowledge plus experience.

Let's put all the cards on the table here. I have fiddled around in the car instead of paying attention to the road. (I get yelled a lot for that by the other half.) I have replaced electrical switches and outlets without turning off the power and I do dabble in plumbing. You may be saying the same thing. After I was done with the above, I would think to myself, "See, it worked out OK." I need to add, THIS TIME. Next time could be a whole different story. Don't ignore the cautions, they are there for a reason. (I would love to think that this little section could save a life or at least a mess.)

Sub-Sorting

As we are getting near the end, I just had to talk a bit about the sub-sorting feature in Excel. I just love it. Say you have a long list of things, the Sub sorter can sort it in alphabetical order, reverse alphabetical order, highest to lowest, lowest to highest and other ways. It allows you to get the information into a format that's most beneficial for you. For example, you have a list of everyone that has hit home runs so far this year in the major leagues. If you want to know a particular person, you can sort alphabetically and look for his name. If you want to see who hit the most or least, you can sort from highest to lowest or vice versa.

This is an extremely important tool for us as we prioritize things in our lives. We have so many things going on and we need a system to make sure we put things in the right order. Let's just look at two aspects of this sub-sorting; importance and timeliness. Just because something is more important, doesn't mean that it necessarily has to be done first. *The combination of these two factors helps us prioritize.*

Your hot water heater is starting to leak around the base just a very little bit. Your kitchen sink leaks water all under the counter because a fitting has broken. If you ask which one is more important, I would assume that you would say the hot water heater because of the work and expense involved compared to a $4.00 PVC fitting. BUT which needs to be done first? I would assume you would say the sink because it is leaking more and messing up the floor under the sink. So, as we prioritize, the sink comes first.

I have heard so many health horror stories about those that put off taking care of health issues because they were too wrapped up with work. So many things today can be treated if identified and treated EARLY. Your wait may make it too late. (Sorry, it was time for a rhyme, get it wait, late, time rhyme…..oh well or as my other half says, WHATEVER) So work is very important, yes. Your career is very important, yes. But if you lose your health, what happens to your career and job?

Prioritizing is sometimes easy to sort but hard to practice. Ann announces,

"We need (review that section) a pool. It's so hot in the summer and it would really help with stress relief and help us get some exercise." Boy, she is good.

"And it will only be $450 a month." Let's ask Ann some questions.

"Do you have at least a couple months of income saved in an emergency fund?"

"Well, not exactly. We do have a little in savings."

"Are you at the maximum on your retirement accounts? Have you started education funds for your children? Ann, are you still there?" I think you get the picture. Importance and timing are crucial elements when we prioritize.

A few years ago, my Dad started asking me to visit him pretty regularly. I live about 5 hours away so I would go up for a weekend as often as I could. Then he asked me to come more often. I had just bought a house and was trying to get it fixed up. (Think long and hard before buying a fixer-upper.) I started in May going up every weekend. I would leave at 6:00 PM or so Friday night and stay till Sunday morning. I just felt like he needed me, so I put off the other things and went up. He was diagnosed with cancer June 1st and died three weeks later. I am so glad I had my priorities straight. Timeliness and importance; the keys to good Sub-sorting. Think objectively, honestly, and examine all the facts, think LONG-TERM and you'll get it right most of the time.

Memory

You'll have to excuse me, I forgot how I was going to start this section off. (Get it; memory... I forgot... hard audience). OK, as far as memory goes, I like to divide it up into two types; working memory and stored memory. Our working memory deals with recalling the things that we need to do our jobs and live our lives. I went to nursing school and I couldn't just place that education back into the deep recesses of my mind. I use the things that I have learned all the time. I have working memory of how to check my oil, pay my bills, balance my checkbook, and hundreds of other things that I need to function properly.

Some things I have tucked away; the things I seldom use. You are probably like me and love talking to people about things that happened years ago. It brings up memories that we have not really forgotten but have put into stored memory and oh, the smiles that come when we say, "Oh ya, I remember that."

Now my mind is kind of weird. (You say "We have read this whole book and totally agree"). Touché! I perfectly remember every word of a poem I learned in second grade, every word. I can tell you Pi is 3.14285714. Now, how do I remember the poem and why can I remember Pi out to 8 places? Now ask me what I had for supper last night? No, please don't.

Here is the importance with memory. There are going to be times in your life when you will need to remember things to make it through. We all know that life is not easy and has many ups and downs. Those of us that have faith, there are going to be times when it is truly tested. We have to remember that we are never alone, we have internal strength to draw from, and that we are not given more than we can handle.

All of us can remember how others have handled their trials. On the lighter side, I get a kick out of people who complain because it is hot out and the electricity was off for 2 hours. I am not making light of your situation, but do you remember the days before we had all air-conditioned homes? I remember getting my first car with A/C. I felt so extravagant.

We should remember the trials, temptations, and heartaches we went through as children while raising ours. Memory enables us to act as guides holding the light and leading the way through their rough patches.

Working memory of course is essential for us to function. You better remember all that is entailed in your job. When I first learned a new job, I took tons of notes but eventually, it will be done by memory. Now, if you work on an assembly line at a cookie factory putting the candy on top of the cookie, I think you got it. If you rebuild transmissions, it is a bit different. When I tear stuff apart to 'fix' it, I often can't remember how to put it all back together. Or I have a couple extra parts which is never good. Thank goodness for camera phones. I use that a lot so I don't tax my memory. (And I also look it up on You Tube).

Imagine having open heart surgery and the surgeon saying, "Now where does this thingy go? I watched the seminar but I just don't remember." Working memory is a must.

Now I want to give you two statements that are so important. I suggest you get the book, 'Reincarnate Now!' as these statements are the premises of the book.

1. Always remember the things you did that produced success as they will be the framework for future success.
2. Always remember the things you did that produced failure and avoid repeating them to incur further failures.

In a nutshell, we have done good things in the past. Perhaps we created some real successes. What was it that made it happen? Was it your determination? Remember then that future successes will need you to be determined. Was it because you worked very hard? Again, hard work will be an ingredient of future successes.

I was the first enlisted medic to take the Advanced Cardiac life support in the European theater in the Air Force. The others in my class were doctors and nurses. I wanted to pass so badly but there was so much to learn and since I hadn't had much exposure to it, I really had to study very hard. I developed a study system. I put questions on the front of 3x5 cards and the answers on the back. I usually put 8-10 questions on each card and I had about a 2 inch stack of cards. It worked; I passed and still used that study method today. I learned from success.

Conversely, what was it that made you fail? Was it because you made a rash decision? Think your decisions out thoroughly. Was it because you reacted hastily? Push the pause button and change your rash reactions to thought out actions. Was it because you gave up and quit? Next time you are fighting an uphill battle, keep fighting and don't ever think of quitting.

We prove to ourselves over and over again that we fail to learn from mistakes. How can you tell? Because we repeat the same mistakes over and over again.

Several years ago, I was cutting some rather wet grass on uneven terrain. I backed up some and slipped. When I did, instead of letting go, I pulled the lawnmower up over my right foot and, you guessed it. I now have 9 and ½ toes. (Could have been a lot worse). A couple of WEEKS ago, I was cutting some rather wet grass in a ditch (uneven terrain) and I backed up and slipped. As soon as I started slipping, I let go of the lawnmower and it shut off and did not roll back on my foot. So, I learned two lessons.

1. I learned that I forgot to be extra careful while cutting wet grass and that backing up was not a good idea.
2. I learned that a past experience reminded me that I needed to consciously let go of the lawnmower. Past failures can be of great value.

Chapter 6

Viruses

Computers can get viruses that can hinder its proper functioning. In our mind, it can keep all the things that we have discussed from opening and working properly. I just want to talk about three of them. I am sure you will be able to think of many more.

Regrets

When I am talking about regrets, I am not talking about you wishing you had done something differently. We all do that. I am talking about being so regretful over your past that you become so unhappy with your present and have a grim outlook for the future. We cannot go back and change past events in our lives because there are no time machines. Living in regret keeps us from living a full life. We are afraid to do anything because we are afraid to fail. When opportunities arise, we see them as opportunities to fail. We have turned our 'I can' into 'I can't.'

I am not going to do it here but please search out articles and excerpts on successful people that had many failures prior to their success. Failure is not final unless you quit. Keep on trying. 'If at first you fail your deed, try again till you succeed'. Abraham Lincoln is a great example of this. Look up all the failures he had in his life. He lost several elections but later went on to become one of our greatest presidents our country has ever had.

I think the classic example though is Thomas Edison. He tried over 2000 things to use for the filament in the light bulb before he found the right one. He told someone that he didn't fail 2000 times, but each time he succeeded in finding that a particular substance *didn't* work. Now that is the attitude to have.

Do you know how the lubricant WD-40 got its name? It was the 40th formula they tried. FOURTY! So, do we regret things, yes but we can't change the past so don't live in regret. As we discussed above, learn from your mistakes and move on to a successful future. The subtitle for the book that I have been telling you to read (Reincarnate Now!) Is 'Yesterday's Storms Can Create Tomorrow's Rainbows'. Think on that for a while and smile. (Oh, another rhyme. No extra charge).

Bitterness – Hatred

This virus has destroyed many computers. Read this very carefully. This virus turns innocent things like anger, disagreements, and disappointments into Bitterness which is only a step away from Hatred. I have heard so many stories and I am sure you have too, about family members that had an argument and since that time haven't spoken to each other. What an unnecessary tragedy! There are two paths you can take from anger; one is, forgive, forget, and restore; the other leads to bitterness and hatred.

I am not primarily talking about huge, life altering events like infidelity or physical abuse, instead I am talking about some of the everyday spats that we get into. A lot of the times it comes from things we do or say as a part of reacting to something else that was said or done. As we mentioned earlier, we need to hit that pause button and think a bit before we react. Life is too short and relationships are too important to let this virus destroy them.

My mother used to get so mad at us. I would be playing with the neighbor boy and we would get into a punch throwing brawl. (We were just 8 – 9 years old). We both would go home dirty and sometimes a little bloody and guess what, my Mom and his Mom would start fighting and we would be in the back yard as best friends again. We were angry but got over it.

People often get angry with family, friends, co-workers, and supervisors. Instead of forgiving and forgetting, they allow the anger to fester like an infection and then it turns to bitterness and hatred. Do you ever wonder what happened to these people that go into their workplace and shoot everyone? I'll tell you what happened; this virus destroyed the normal thinking processes of their minds.

How can people go into a church full of people that belong to one race and start shooting? How can someone strap a bomb on themselves and blow it up in the midst of people of a certain nationality? How could people orchestrate an attack that saw planes flying into buildings killing thousands of people? Their hatred is so intense that their computers are totally defiled by the virus.

Do me a favor. If you have a strained relationship with someone because you are harboring bitterness, at least consider taking that first step toward restoration. I have had short periods of strained relationships and it sure feels good to get back together again; especially if you took the first step. Go ahead; make that call. Go ahead, I'll wait. How did it go? See, I told you!

Discouragement

In a minute, I am going to tell you about the 'Discouragement Cycle'. It is a cycle that spirals down and believe me, you don't want to be on it. Some discouraged people need counseling and other medical treatments and if you need this, I highly recommend that you do. I think at times all of us get a bit discouraged. Sometimes it is caused by terrible things that have happened in our lives, sometimes failures and sometimes it's just because we can't see any hope of a better future.

Discouragement should not be a permanent part of your life. Something happens, you get discouraged; get over it and move on. Life is too short and you need all of you to function properly to win in this game called life. All my life I wanted to be a doctor, but it just never worked out. Think about that; I failed at achieving a major goal in my life. I could be discouraged 24-7 over that but I chose to move on. I am a nurse, a father, a grandfather, and the author of two tremendous books so far. (I hear you laughing at that)

If you look at the word itself and break it down; **dis** – means without / and **courage**. In other words, you lost your courage; courage to move on and try new things, courage to work towards another goal, courage to love again, and courage to face upcoming days after a tragedy. When you get discouraged, you begin to sort things differently. You're not happy that your glass is half full, you're discouraged because it's half empty. I really believe that in order to live a successful life you have to;

- Believe in yourself.
- Have the energy to get you going.
- Have the fight in you to face battles.
- Have hope in you so you can keep your eyes on the prize.
- Have determination to keep on going and never quit.

Guess what? When you are discouraged, you lose all of that. The discouragement cycle goes like this. You get discouraged, and then because you are discouraged, you lose all the things above and become so anemic you cannot function. Because you can't function, you don't get anything done. And because you don't get anything done, yep, you get even more discouraged and the cycle continues.

How do you break that cycle? The laws of motion fit in so well here. *Objects at rest will remain at rest until acted upon by another force.* To get going you need another force. There are several forces that can get us going: passion, desire, serving others, devotion, and just plain old will power.

On the other hand, *objects in motion will remain in motion until acted upon by another force.* Once you get going, you will keep going until you let discouragement come back and stop you. Get moving, you can do it.

When discouragement and depression set in, it can seem related to things that have happened in the past but it is really about facing the days ahead. My oldest son died unexpectedly at 21 years old for no apparent cause. I was crushed as was the rest of the family. I hurt so badly that I couldn't stand it. How can I possibly live with this? I had no idea how I would ever be able to make it through another day. But I did; then another; then a week, month…… that happened back in 1999.

I learned several valuable lessons. One was; when tragedy hits, you can't see too far down the road. You have to take one step at a time and then you can see a bit further.

Conclusion

I try to write all my books in a very informal manner so we can just kind of have a chat. (You know, I talk and you listen and ask questions. Although I can't hear your questions, BUT I am sure they are good ones). My main goal is to give you some things that can help your life in some way or other. I often read books and perhaps just get a few nuggets that will help but it is certainly worth the read. (Better than what is on TV) I certainly hope you have gotten some things from this book that will make your life better, and that you will share the concepts with others. The most valuable treasures are the treasures we can share.

Our mind is a wonderful thing. It controls everything. Control what goes in there, and make sure you consciously place everything in the right folder. Make sure you are watching the young little computers running around the house as well. Take advantage of the accessories and watch out for the viruses. You can have wonderful stability in your life by sub-sorting (prioritizing) correctly.

Take an audit of all the things you do subconsciously and make sure you have a good decision-making process. Pay special attention to the things that you deem as important. You will find that the decisions you make to serve others will yield great happiness. Restoring broken relationships is so cool and do not get near that discouragement cycle. I certainly wish you all the best.

Printed in the United States
By Bookmasters